Discovering Purpose

Finding God's Plan For Your Life

RANDALL RITTENBERRY

Discovering Purpose

Finding God's Plan For Your Life

ISBN: 978-0-578-70138-7

Printed in the United States of America

Copyright © 2019 by Randall Rittenberry

Compass Publishing
USA

Acknowledgments

This particular project has been a long time in coming. I have worked on this book off and on for 20 years! The original manuscript was dated July 9th, 1999. The rough draft was completed on June 27th, 2019. I am writing this on July 6th, 2019. God doesn't give up, and neither should we!

I would like to thank my wife, Cynthia, first of all. She has been my biggest supporter, and cheerleader, especially over these last couple of months. She knows my passion for this more than any other person, and understands it as she has seen how finding my purpose has transformed every aspect of my life.

To my friend, Rich Stevens: thank you for being in my corner, and for your support. It is appreciated more than you know.

To my friend, Ron Marquardt: who never allowed me to walk away from my purpose.

To my friend, Mary Dorian: who believes in me and tells me that every chance she gets.

To my pastor, Ron Allen and his wife Beth: for investing in a young man full of insecurity and stubbornness, and for speaking into my life.

Table of Contents

Chapter 1

The Importance of Finding Purpose

What is the meaning of life? Why am I here? Is there more to life than this? Regardless of the many time periods, cultures, and societies that have existed these questions have been pondered, and debated, in them all. The search for meaning and purpose is a common thread that binds all of humanity, past and present. Proverbs 29:18 gives us a great insight into the importance of finding purpose:

Where there is no vision, the people perish . . .

Without a sense of purpose our heart will be dissatisfied. Since the issues of life flow from our heart[1], if our heart is dissatisfied, our lives will be as well. That dissatisfaction will be reflected in every part of our lives. I see this all the time when speaking with people; they jump from thing to thing with no stability or direction, and they remain miserable throughout their entire life. Their misery then pours out to those around them, which then creates chaos in relationships. It also leads to confusion and turmoil in their minds and emotions. It can

The Importance of Finding Purpose

even lead to sickness.

Prov. 13:12a Hope deferred makes the heart sick[2] . . .

(author's note - all of life flows from the heart:: see note 1.)

Purpose is important to keep our lives stable and on point. It is similar to the rudder on a ship. Without the rudder, we will just drift wherever the wind takes us. With a rudder, we can steer our ship toward the destination we see in our heart. Look at what Proverbs 29:18 says from two other translations:

TMB   If people can't see what God is doing, they stumble all over themselves

NIV   Where there is no revelation, the people cast off restraint. . .

Identifying our purpose helps us to steer our lives. It keeps us focused. It gives us a sense of value. When we do not pursue our purpose or if we lose sight of it, we will stumble in life. Notice the *NIV* says when we have no revelation of our purpose, we cast off restraint. If we feel purposeless, we will have actions that correspond to that belief of having no purpose.

The two places where great destinies can tragically end are prison and the grave. People go to the grave prematurely, sometimes, because they feel they have no purpose; so they give in to destructive behaviors that cut their lives short. When there is no sense of value, then any behavior is permissible. There is no regard to the consequence of destructive decisions. How many lives have been cut short because of over-indulgence, or lack of restraint? People in prison also develop and give in to destructive behaviors that distract and derail them. Because they cannot see their true purpose they head down a path of instinct and uncontrolled emotions. They are responding to something; they are just not sure what it is, and they do not know what to do with what they are feeling on the inside.

We see this with the story of Moses. We know from the book of Exodus that Moses was given up at birth by his mother to save his life. He was found by the pharaoh's daughter and raised in the pharaoh's household. One day, after Moses was grown, he witnessed an Egyptian slave driver beating a fellow Hebrew. Moses ended up killing the Egyptian[3]. This is a perfect illustration of someone who responded to a God-given purpose in a destructive way, who did not think about the consequences of that action.

Acts 7:23-25 NIV   When Moses was forty years old, he decided to visit his fellow Israelites. He saw one of them being mistreated by an Egyptian, so he went to his defense and avenged him by killing the Egyptian. Moses thought that his own people would realize that God was using him to rescue them, but they did not.

Moses felt a sense of purpose; he desired to set his people free. Because he did not know what to do with that sense of purpose, he responded with murder. He went down a path of instinct and uncontrolled emotions. I would call murder a destructive behavior! We will see this later as well, but that one destructive decision put off his purpose for forty years! We can also see this reflected throughout history. The atrocities committed throughout history result directly from men and women corrupting their purpose.

We need not look back very far to see this. A great example to look at in the not too distant past is Adolf Hitler. Hitler was obviously a leader but became destructive because he did not properly identify his purpose; nor could he see his personal value and worth besides trying to conquer, or trying to exterminate an entire race of people. Purpose keeps us from destructive behaviors. When we know our purpose, we will have actions that correspond to that purpose. Our actions will lead us on a path toward our purpose. We no longer live without value, and we do not cast off restraint. With a sense of purpose the realization sets in that certain behaviors will prevent us from reaching our destiny.

Serendipity

Purpose opens up a whole world of possibilities you never considered before. Once you find your main purpose, you will find other opportunities attached to that purpose. I would compare it to a wheel: your main purpose is the hub, but then spokes come out of the hub. The spokes are the opportunities that develop from the main purpose or hub. Once I found that my purpose was to teach, new ideas sprang out of that purpose. Writing, traveling, and other types of speaking opportunities were a few of the 'spokes' that came out of the 'hub', the purpose.

Finding purpose makes the possibilities for your life limitless. It presents a different way of viewing life. It is the 'law of serendipity'. Serendipity is what I find along the way to my goal, or purpose. I may be walking into the grocery store; the store is my goal. Between my car and the store, I find a $100 bill. I wasn't looking for the $100 bill, but I found it on the way to the store, my goal. It was an unexpected by-product of walking to my goal. The 'law of serendipity' leads us into unlimited potential. We just must simply respond to opportunity. There are always opportunities on the road to discovering purpose.

The Roadmap

Knowing our purpose also eliminates a lot of confusion about decisions. If I know my purpose, decisions come easier because I am deciding based on how it will affect where I am going. With any decision that comes I simply must ask myself: will this add to or take away from my purpose? Not long after realizing my purpose I was presented with a job opportunity better than what I was in. I thought about it and prayed about it for several days.

I finally decided not to take the job. The reason I did not take it was because it would take away from my purpose. It would lead me to a different destination than the one I saw in my heart. It would not have allowed me to do the things I needed to do to prepare for my destiny. Could God have gotten me there anyway? Yes! But it would have delayed me in the same way as Moses' destiny was delayed.

Purpose provides a roadmap for our lives. If we are unsure about a decision we can reference the roadmap. Will the decision we make take us off the road to our destiny, or will it take us closer to reaching the destination we see in our hearts? Will this decision allow me to follow God toward my destination, or will it become a stumbling block that takes me away from my kingdom purpose? Will this decision corrupt my purpose, or strengthen my purpose?

Does this mean I can never make a mistake? Does it mean God cannot help me if I make a bad decision? Absolutely not! I am not saying that one mistake will forever condemn you. What I am saying is that applying this concept will help you in your journey; it will alleviate some potential problems. Just as we can look at a map and know to turn left or right toward our goal, we can also use purpose to determine the direction of our decisions. This concept alone can help keep us from confusion. It will keep us from being 'wishy-washy', and it keeps us from being tossed back and forth by the winds of life and our emotions.

The main thing I want you to see is that finding your purpose is important! You do not have to settle with a purposeless life. God has a purpose for you! We want to believe there is a greater purpose for our life. The good news is that God has given us a purpose. What is that purpose? That seems to be the hard part for each of us: identifying what our kingdom purpose is, and how to get there.

In the chapters to come we will look at some factors that will help us to find God's plan and purpose for our lives. We will weed through some misconceptions of destiny and God's will. We will learn biblical principles for fulfilling that purpose. We will see he has truly given us a hope and a future[4]!

Chapter 2

Honor and Dignity

Mankind, even from ancient times, has realized there is a creator. Each ancient culture developed a philosophy that tried to explain a creator. The Chinese had the tao. The Greeks had the logos. Other cultures had mythologies of multiple deities. These ancient people, although they believed a creator existed, could not grasp how God intended for man to relate to Him.

Their philosophies were these cultures' attempt to explain God, and their attempt to explain how we relate to God. Each philosophy, even though from different cultures, had a common thread. They were impersonal and implied that God was distant and unconcerned with the affairs of mankind. We see in Genesis, Chapter 2, verses 7-8, what God has always intended for man:

NKJV   And the LORD God formed man of the dust of the ground. And breathed into his nostrils the breath of life; and man became a living being. The LORD God planted a garden eastward in Eden, and where He put the man whom He had formed.

The word 'formed' above means to fashion as a potter does clay[1]. It implies intimacy and love. It shows us that God made man by His own hands. Genesis Chapter One states he **created** or made everything else. This shows that God placed a higher worth on mankind than he did on the rest of creation. He was personally involved with us. We are the only things made in the image of God. We are the only things made to have fellowship with God. We are given a place of honor and dignity above all of creation. We were not made by chance, or by a random sequence of events. It is vital for us to grab this concept so we can find, and fulfill, our purpose. If we do not grasp God's value for us, then we will not see the value of the purpose He has given us.

Gen. 2:15 (KJV) And the LORD God took the man, and put him into the garden of Eden to dress it and to keep it.

We see here in verse 15 that God put Adam in the garden to **dress** and to **keep** it. In other words, God gave Adam something to do. He had a **purpose** for Adam. The word 'dress' means *to work and till*[2]. Adam was to work, or maintain, the garden. He was also supposed to **keep** the garden. 'Keep' means *to guard*[3]. So Adam's purpose was to work and guard what God had given to him. He was also supposed to have a relationship with God. Genesis Chapter 3, verse 8, says that God walked in the garden in the cool of the day. This implies that he had a relationship with Adam. In verse 9, God calls to Adam. He obviously was used to speaking with Adam and being with him at this time of day. So part of man's purpose is the work that God has for us to do, but the other part of man's purpose is to have a relationship with God. We can see this dual purpose from Hebrews Chapter 2, verses 5-7:

KJV For unto the angels has he not put in subjection the world to come, whereof we speak. But one in a certain place testified, saying, **What** *is man, that you are mindful of him? or the son of man, that you* **visit** *him? You made him a little lower than the angels[4]; You crowned him with* **glory and honor**, *and did* **set him over the works of your hands.**

The word 'visit' implies a caring relationship, a fellowship[5]. Then we see how God crowned mankind with 'glory and honor', which means dignity and worth[6]. What was the glory and honor, dignity and worth we received? It was being set over the care of creation, according to the end of verse 7. So the conclusion from this is God valued us enough to care for us, fellowship with us, and give us a purpose.

Genesis Chapter 3 then records the 'fall of man'. When this happened, two things took place. First, in verse 7, Adam and Eve experienced shame. They saw they were naked and covered themselves. They were ashamed of their nakedness. In Genesis Chapter 2, verse 25, they were both naked, but not ashamed. They saw themselves differently; they saw themselves as though they were without glory and honor; as though they had no value, or were without dignity and worth.

The second thing that happened, we see in verse 8, was that Adam and Eve became afraid of God. They were not afraid of him before 'the fall' happened. Ever since this event, man has been ashamed of himself, which has led to the wrong kind of fear of God. True Biblical fear means a reverential worship of God, not a fear of punishment[7]. The wrong kind of fear of God caused Adam and Eve to hide from God[8]. Shame prevented Adam from taking responsibility for his actions[9], which put him off of his purpose.

Fear and shame are the by-products of not seeing ourselves with dignity, honor, and value. Ultimately, this fear and shame kept Adam from fulfilling his purpose. That is why it is so important to be established in the dignity, honor, and value that God has for us; if we do not see our value, we will live in fear and shame. This will create two possibilities in us: the first possibility is that we will not fulfill our purpose, just like Adam. The second possibility is that we could find our purpose, but try to find our value from the purpose rather than from God.

It is a paradox: knowing we have a purpose will help to give us a sense of value; but, the source of our value must come from how God sees us; through the dignity and honor with which He created us. We can never supplant a relationship with God, being in His presence, for our accomplishments. Then we simply are using our purpose to hide from Him; yet all the while giving ourselves a false sense of worth and value.

Results of Fear and Shame

The fear and shame that resulted from the 'fall of man' has led mankind over the centuries to search for a meaning to life apart from God. Because we do not believe God has value for us, and has given us a purpose for our lives, we therefore must look to ourselves or to something else for purpose. This search has led mankind into various philosophies and ideas. These philosophies and ideas are actually just ways we try to hide from God; just like Adam did because of fear and shame.

One idea that mankind has embraced is the theory of evolution. Evolution says that random events have caused us to reach our present stage of existence and development. The danger of embracing evolution, in any form, is that it leads us to believe either there is no God or that God has placed no value on us. It says that if there is a God, He set the universe in motion to evolve at random. If we exist only by chance then maybe dogs could have evolved into humans. It takes away all of the dignity and honor that God gave to us. This philosophy, through the years, has helped lend to the belief that our lives are worthless. If we do not believe that God created us for a specific purpose, and to have fellowship with, then we have no choice but to believe that we have no value.

On the other side of the coin, there is tradition and religion. Religion has told us that God created us, but that His purpose for us could bring us pain and misery. Tradition says that God wants us to serve Him in things we will not enjoy. According to tradition and religion, we must accept any pain and misery as God using us as part of a scheme in His grand plan. This also takes away from the value God has for us by saying we are nothing more than chess pieces, or at best, puppets being controlled by the grand puppeteer. It is a very cold and impersonal view of God. Religion and tradition have caused people to be afraid of seeking God for their purpose. We are afraid that we will 'miss it', which may make God angry at us; or we are afraid that we will have to do something that will make us miserable. Because of this we do not even attempt to find our purpose. This is the same result that the theory of evolution produces in us. The truth, according to God's word, is that he deems mankind more valuable than anything else that He has created[10].

A God-Sense of Worth and Value

In Genesis, Chapter One, we see God creating the earth and everything on it and in it. After creating plants, birds, fish, the sun and the moon, God looked at it and said it was good. When he created or formed mankind, God looked at mankind and said it was **very** good[11]. How God views us is that we make what he created better. Everything he created was perfect, but we made it even better. That is the view that God has of each of us personally.

When we have a God-sense of value it will produce in us a sense of purpose. It takes away any shame we carry about ourselves; the removing of shame allows us to embrace the purpose God has for us. It will also take away any fear of allowing God to lead us and guide us.

Why would we fear someone with such great value for us? Why would we be afraid to go where He leads? When we have no God-sense of value we will feel purposeless. We discussed the effects of that way of thinking in the last chapter, regarding behavior; but there is another possible result of this way of thinking: we could easily become subject to the delusion of man's approval. We could fall prey to replacing God's purpose with other men's agendas. We will seek approval, which lends to our feeling of worth, from somewhere. If we do not feel as though God values us, we will then turn to other people for that sense of value.

The danger of that possibility is that men's whims are like the wind: subject to change in an instant. If we become co-dependent on others, then we are at the mercy of their emotions and perceptions. It is a very unsafe place to live. It is much better to build a God-sense of value; He never changes! Not only does He never change, He does not alter His opinion enough to cast a shadow!

*James 1:17 NIV Every good and perfect gift is from above, coming down from the Father of the heavenly lights, **who does not change** like shifting shadows.*

*NKJV Every good gift and every perfect gift is from above, and comes down from the Father of lights, with whom there is **no variation or shadow** of turning.*

That is where we want to get our worth: from God Himself. If we try to get our value from any place other than from God, our lives will be unstable; the reason is because any other source we may try to attain value from is unstable. God is the only source of worth and value from

19

which we will have stability, and it is from that stability we can build our lives toward our purpose!

Chapter 3

The Power of Hope

I do not want to just give you information, but I want to empower you to apply this information to your life. I want to give you the keys to finding your purpose, but without an understanding of this one principle, those keys will be useless. The power to pursue our dreams, even when the going gets tough, is in hope. Hope is not wishing something would happen. I hear people say things like "I hope I get that job" or "I hope everything will work out". What they are really saying is it might happen, but it might not happen. This is not the kind of hope we find in the scriptures. Biblical **hope** is a *confident expectation of good things from God*[1]. Jeremiah 29:11, in the King James Version of the Bible, speaks of an *expected end*, or the expectation (hope) of a good end. Let's look at this verse in a different translation:

NLT "For I know the plans I have for you," says the LORD. "They are plans for good and not for disaster, to give you a future and a hope."

Notice how this version translates 'an expected end' to 'a future and a hope'. God has given each of us hope for our life; a good end we can expect. Notice that He says that His plans are not to harm us, but to prosper us. For hope to come alive in me, I must believe that He is good, and His intentions toward me are good. When hope comes alive, I will not be afraid that God will withhold my dreams from me. He gave me the dream (hope), and He will help me to fulfill it.

Rom. 8:31-32 KJV What shall we then say to these things? If God be for us, who can be against us? He that spared not his own Son, but delivered him up for us all, how shall he not with him also freely give us all things?

This also means I will not be afraid that man can take my dream, and my future, from me. The main reason we do not pursue our dreams is because of fear; both of God, and of men. This is why Moses fled to the wilderness when he killed the Egyptian. He was afraid that he would be killed by the Pharaoh for his actions (fear of man). If Moses could have grabbed onto hope, he would not have fled. Hope, or confident expectation of good, would have caused Moses to realize that since God was calling him then God could also protect him and deliver him.

So Moses became afraid that man would kill him and afraid that God would not protect him. In the short time between the slaying of the Egyptian and fleeing into the desert, Moses probably experienced a lot of emotions. 1 John 4:18 says that fear has torment. Fear torments our minds, and our emotions: our soul. The word 'soul' in the New Testament is the Greek word psuche[2], which means our mind, will, and emotions. It is where we get the words *psyche* and *psychology*. So if Moses fled due to fear then his soul (mind, will, emotions) was tormented.

Two things overcome fear: hope and love.

*1 John 4:18 KJV   There is no fear in love; **but perfect love casts out fear:** because fear has torment. He that fears is not made perfect in love.*

*Heb. 6:18-19 NIV   God did this so that, by two unchangeable things in which it is impossible for God to lie, we who have fled to take hold of the **hope** offered to us may be greatly encouraged. We have this **hope as an anchor for the soul,** firm and secure. It enters the inner sanctuary behind the curtain.*

Hope and love work hand-in-hand. Notice Heb. 6:19 says that hope (confident expectation of good) anchors the soul, or *psuche.* When I know that God wants good for me it causes stability to come to my mind. It causes peace to come to my mind. I know that as I walk out God's plan that He is there cheering me on[3]. He is working to cause good things to come to me. The only way I can know He wants good for me, however, is to know that He loves me. God is a perfect father. A good earthly father wants his children to succeed beyond even their own imaginations. How much more does our heavenly Father want us to succeed?

Matt. 7:9-11 NIV   Which of you, if his son asks for bread, will give him a stone? Or if he asks for a fish, will give him a snake? If you, then, though you are evil, know how to give good gifts to your children, how much more will your Father in heaven give good gifts to those who ask him!

When we become convinced of God's love for us then hope comes alive in us, and empowers us to fulfill our purpose. Hope will become the factor that motivates us to continue despite obstacles. Obstacles will come, but hope will keep us moving forward. The hope we have in

God's love, and in our purpose, has to be what propels us toward our destiny. We cannot trust in our circumstances or in the opinions and actions of others.

Let's look at Moses again. It is interesting to note that even though Moses knew his expected end, his Hebrew brethren did not recognize the call of God on his life. In Exodus 2:13, Moses tries to break up a fight between two Hebrews. This was the call of God, or expected end, on Moses' life to be the judge of Israel; we see this come to pass in Exodus 18:13-16[4]. Notice the reaction that the man in the wrong had toward Moses in Exodus 2:13-14:

NIV   The next day he went out and saw two Hebrews fighting. He asked the one in the wrong, "Why are you hitting your fellow Hebrew?" The man said, "Who made you ruler and judge over us? Are you thinking of killing me as you killed the Egyptian?" Then Moses was afraid and thought, "What I did must have become known."

Moses was trying to do what God had called him to do, but this man did not see it. Moses assumed everyone knew what God called him to do.

*Acts 7:23-25   NIV   "When Moses was forty years old, he decided to visit his fellow Israelites. He saw one of them being mistreated by an Egyptian, so he went to his defense and avenged him by killing the Egyptian. Moses thought that his own people would realize that God was using him to rescue them, **but they did not.***

Sometimes we are just like Moses. We assume that everyone sees, and knows, the call that God has put on our life. People do not automatically know our expected end and will not always agree with what we say God wants. It is something we must walk out and prove by being faithful and determined. Often it would be easier to run away like Moses did. In times like this we must trust in hope. We must continue on even when others do not agree with our hope.

We must be the same way regarding our circumstances as well. How many dreams and destinies have died in the history of mankind because circumstances have been regarded more than the hope of God and His promises? I would say untold thousands. Circumstances can never be allowed to be the deciding factor in whether we fulfill our purpose or not. We have a great biblical example in the story of Abraham. The scriptures tell us that Abraham believed in hope, even when in the natural there was no hope.

Rom. 4:18-21 NIV ***Against all hope, Abraham believed in hope*** *and so became the father of many nations, just as it had been said to him, "So shall your offspring be." Without weakening in his faith, he faced the fact that his body was as good as dead—since he was about a hundred years old—and that Sarah's womb was also dead. Yet* ***he did not waver through unbelief regarding the promise of God,*** *but was strengthened in his faith and gave glory to God,* ***being fully persuaded that God had power to do what he had promised.***

Again, let's look at Moses. When God came to Moses and called him to lead the Israelites out of Egypt Moses argued with him about his circumstances. With every argument, however, God had an answer for Moses[5]. He was giving Moses hope, or confident expectation, beyond the circumstances. We must be able to see hope beyond our circumstances and beyond the opinions of men. We must trust in the hope that God has for us. The power of hope will keep us pushing forward to see our purpose fulfilled!

Chapter 4

A Common Thread

Jer. 29:11 KJV For I know the thoughts that I think toward you, says the LORD, thoughts of peace, and not of evil, to give you an expected end.

Inside of every person there is a sense of purpose. There is a longing within each of us to fulfill that purpose. I believe that everything we do is a by-product of trying to fulfill that desire in us. Some people try to fulfill that longing with drugs. Some try to fulfill it with money or social status. Others try to fulfill that desire with unhealthy, or co-dependent, relationships. Every human being wants their life to be part of a greater purpose. Each of us wants more than just to go to work, come home, eat, sleep, wake up, go to work, come home, eat, sleep, etc., etc.

The greater purpose we are looking for is what Jeremiah 29:11 calls an *expected end.* That expected end is the plan that God has for us; the goal He expects for us to achieve. We spent our childhood playing games of 'What I Want To Be When I Grow Up'. The things we dreamt of as children may have changed from day to day, but a common thread ran through each dream. For example, one day a child may want to be a policeman; the next day that same child may want to be a fireman. These are two different vocations, yet both are protectors and rescuers of people. This is the expected end that God has for that child; to be a rescuer and protector of people.

This is one way for us to determine what our purpose is: by looking at the common thread of our dreams, even from childhood. When I was seeking God for my purpose, this is one tool that He used to help guide me towards my calling. He took the dreams I had, even as a child, and showed me the common thread woven through each of them. When I was five years old a man asked me what I wanted to be when I grew up. What was my answer? I told him I wanted to be a preacher!

As I grew older, I played sports. My dream, at age 9 or 10, was to be a professional baseball player. I would travel and be in front of people. Everyone would see me as I walked on the field; they would know my name. Around age 13 my dream was to be a professional football player. I would travel and be in front of people. Everyone would see me as I walked on the field; they would know my name. At age 16 my dream was to be a rock star! I would travel and be in front of people. Everyone would see me as I walked on the stage; they would know my name.

What was the common thread in all of that? I wanted to travel and be in front of people. I wanted to have influence. What God showed me was that it was always his plan for me to travel and be in front of people. I had simply taken the desire I had at age 5 to be a preacher and redirected it towards other pursuits. The common thread, however, remained. We see the concept of the common thread in the book of Exodus and the life of Moses.

In Exodus Chapter 1 the Egyptian king told the Hebrew midwives to kill the males that were born to the Hebrews but to spare the females. In this way the Egyptian king sought to diminish the Hebrew population. The Hebrew midwives feared God and saved the male Hebrew babies in direct defiance of the pharaoh's orders. When the king asked why the males were being saved, the Hebrew midwives responded by saying that the males were born before the midwives arrived. So the pharaoh ordered the males to be thrown into the river. (Exodus 1:15-22)

In Exodus Chapter 2 we see the account of a Hebrew woman who gave birth to a son. The woman hid her son for three months. She then realized she could not hide him any longer. So she fixed a basket for the child, placed him inside, and set the basket into the river. The pharaoh's daughter saw the basket and opened it. She realized it was one of the Hebrew babies and decided to raise him as her own child. (Exodus 2:1-9) Then we see this in verse 10:

*Ex. 2:10 When the child grew older, she took him to Pharaoh's daughter and he became her son. She named him Moses, saying, "I **drew him out** of the water."*

The phrase 'drew out' also means brought forth[1]. Moses was *brought forth* from the water; his name meant 'to *bring forth*' and he was to *bring forth,* or 'draw out', his people from Egypt. This was Moses' *expected end.*

As we will see it became the common thread in the events of his life. Moses knew he was to lead Israel out of Egypt[2]. Moses wanted to help his people so desperately that he even killed an Egyptian slave driver beating a fellow Hebrew.

Ex. 2:11-12 NIV   One day, after Moses had grown up, he went out to where his own people were and watched them at their hard labor. He saw an Egyptian beating a Hebrew, one of his own people. Glancing this way and that and seeing no one, he killed the Egyptian and hid him in the sand.

The account of this event in Moses' life ends with the pharaoh trying to kill him. So Moses ran away from Egypt into Midian, which was considered the wilderness[3]. Now let's look at what happened when Moses arrived at Midian. This event happens in chapter 2 also, in verses 16-19:

*NIV   Now a priest of Midian had seven daughters, and they came to draw water and fill the troughs to water their father's flock. Some shepherds came along and drove them away, but Moses got up and **came to their rescue** and watered their flock. When the girls returned to Reuel their father, he asked them, "Why have you returned so early today?" They answered, "An Egyptian rescued us from the shepherds. He even **drew water** for us and watered the flock."*

Moses was still trying to deliver and rescue people; he couldn't escape the desire, the expected end. That common thread was with him wherever he went. Notice, in verse 19, that the man's daughters said that Moses "drew water for us." Moses was not only delivering and rescuing them, he even 'drew out', or *brought forth*, water to give to the animals. There is no escaping the common thread or *expected end*.

You will lean toward it even if you don't realize it.

Look at your life and find the common thread that runs through your dreams. There is a common thread, or theme, that runs through each of our lives. That common thread is a clue to your purpose.

Chapter 5

Heart's Desire

*Psalm 37:4 KJV   Delight yourself also in the LORD; and he shall give you
the **desires of your heart**.*

O ne key we overlook when trying to determine our purpose
is the desires of our own heart. Religion and tradition
have made the 'desires of your heart' a derogatory term. From that
perspective, it is something to be shunned and condemned. The
argument is we should be trying to find God's will, not ours. Religion
and tradition portray our desires as a bad, evil thing. It is a 'suffering
for the kingdom' mentality. The thinking is that if you enjoy what you
are doing then it is not God's will. It is viewed through the perspective
of suffering and sacrifice, not joy. But a desire can be a good thing:

*1 Timothy 3:1 KJV   This is a true saying, If a man **desire** the office of a
bishop, he **desires** a good work.*

In this verse, Paul tells Timothy that to desire to be a bishop is a good thing. He is saying desire can equal good. Not all desires are bad. Let's be honest here: God will not give us desires that are crooked. It would hurt us, and He loves us too much to hurt us. If we are to fulfill our purpose, it will be a joy to us.

Proverbs 10:22 KJV The blessing of the LORD, it maketh rich, and he addeth no sorrow with it.

If it is of God, it will be a delight to us regardless of the price. Is there sacrifice involved? Yes, but even that will bring us joy because we know we are on the path to our *expected end*. Whatever God brings to us, even our calling and purpose, He does not add sorrow to it. Religion and tradition say whatever you do not want to do that is what God wants you to do. Our desires are to be set aside for His desires. But what if the desires in our heart are simply a reflection of His will in us?

We must look at the desires of our heart to help us find our purpose. In Psalm 37:4, it says He will give us the desires of our heart. What does that mean? The word 'give' in this verse has two meanings: *give (or bring)* and *make (or put)[1]*. He not only gives, or brings, us our desires, but He also makes our desires. He puts them in us. If it is something you want to do it is because God gave you the desire to do it. Our purpose in life is a desire of our heart that God put in us from birth.

Jeremiah 1:5 KJV Before I formed thee in the belly I knew thee; and before thou camest forth out of the womb I sanctified thee, and I ordained thee a prophet unto the nations.

From this we can see that our desires, good desires, reflect God's will. They are a picture of the *expected end*. The word 'formed' in this verse is the same word as we saw in Genesis 2 when God **formed** Adam[2]. The word 'ordained' is the same word as 'give' in Psalm 37:4[3]. The word 'sanctified' means to prepare, to appoint[4]. One meaning of the word 'knew' is *care*[5]. He formed you, gave you a desire, and appointed you to it because He cares for you. He ordained you, gave you a purpose from birth; really while you were still in the womb! That desire will push everything you do in life, consciously or subconsciously. To dismiss those desires, or to overlook them, is doing the same to your God-given purpose. There will always be a part of you that feels incomplete until you look into those desires. Even if you are walking in your purpose to some degree, neglecting this aspect is limiting the vision and plan for your life.

Proverbs 13:12 KJV Hope deferred maketh the heart sick: but when the **desire** *cometh, it is a tree of life.*

Natural Tendencies

Part of identifying your heart desires is to look at your natural tendencies. It is very similar to the common thread we saw in the last chapter. It will be the things you lean towards in every situation, in every phase of your life. It is the default button of your life. Your heart will always bring you to situations where your desire resides. It is in your spiritual DNA. It happens when you are not aware of it, and even when you are aware of it. How often have you said or thought 'It seems like I am always doing this.'? "I always find myself (fill in the

Heart's Desire

blank)." It happens with a lot more regularity than you think.

Leaders always find themselves in areas of leadership; helpers always find a way to help; teachers always teach. It is just who they **are**. No matter how hard we try at times to avoid those situations, we are always drawn back.

Proverbs 18:16 KJV   A man's gift maketh room for him, and bringeth him before great men.

The word 'brings' here can mean lead[6]. This implies that your gift, the desire, the hope, the *expected end* is always leading you. We saw this with Moses in Midian at the well after he fled Egypt. Was it simply coincidence that Moses came upon those women at the well? Or was it his heart, full of the desire God had put in him, leading him into that situation?

*Proverbs 16:9 KJV A man's **heart** deviseth his way: but the LORD directeth his steps.*

No matter how hard we try, we cannot get away from the pull of our natural tendencies. I know. I have tried. I would try to walk away from my purpose, give it all up. Yet, the Lord continued to pull me back through the desire in my heart; the desire He placed in me when He formed me. He used it to direct my steps. I can honestly say I am more content following my purpose than when I was not following it.

Seeing From The Heart

Another key to discovering purpose often overlooked is our dreams, and daydreams. Remember, Proverbs 16:9 says a man's heart devises his way. The NIV says that humans plan their own course[7]. We have established that the desire is put there by God when He formed us. Because of that, our heart will show us the blueprint of that plan in different ways. One way is where our imagination takes us in those moments when we allow ourselves to dream. I call this 'seeing from the heart'. We see this in the life of Joseph:

Genesis 37:3-11 CEV Jacob loved Joseph more than he did any of his other sons, because Joseph was born after Jacob was very old. Jacob had given Joseph a fancy coat to show that he was his favorite son, and so Joseph's brothers hated him and would not be friendly to him. One day, Joseph told his brothers what he had dreamed, and they hated him even more. Joseph said, "Let me tell you about my dream. We were out in the field, tying up bundles of wheat. Suddenly my bundle stood up, and your bundles gathered around and bowed down to it." His brothers asked, "Do you really think you are going to be king and rule over us?" Now they hated Joseph more than ever because of what he had said about his dream. Joseph later had another dream, and he told his brothers, "Listen to what else I dreamed. The sun, the moon, and eleven stars bowed down to me." When he told his father about this dream, his father became angry and said, "What's that supposed to mean? Are your mother and I and your brothers all going to come and bow down in front of you?" Joseph's brothers were jealous of him, but his father kept wondering about the dream.

Joseph saw his destiny in those **dreams**! We then see in Gen. 42:6[8], and again in Gen. 43:26[9], that Joseph's dreams came to pass. Joseph did not see all of the details of what would happen to him. He had a glimpse of what was to come, *the expected end*. A man's heart devises his ways, but the Lord directs his steps[10]. There are so many lessons from Joseph's life. But what we want to focus on right now is the vision from his heart that came in dreams.

I consider daydreams to be a part of this as well. Some would say that daydreams are the inventions of fools, or simply selfish ambition. Remember what I said earlier in this chapter: not all desires, or ambitions, are bad[11]. When seeking God, He can speak to your heart in this way. He will give a glimpse of an image, or a whisper, showing and saying how He sees you in your *expected end*. Ideas you could never imagine on your own will take shape. When you delight yourself in the Lord, He gives you the desires of your heart[12]. There is no limit in Him. Look at Abram (Abraham):

Genesis 13:14-15 NLT   After Lot had gone, the LORD said to Abram, "Look as far as you can see in every direction—north and south, east and west. I am giving all this land, as far as you can see, to you and your descendants as a permanent possession.

Notice the Lord told Abram He would give him 'everything he could see'. He was trying to get Abram to see beyond his own limitations. He was showing Abram how to see from his heart. He wanted him to see the possibilities, not only for his own life, but of his descendants. This is exactly how He uses daydreams with us. That is what Abram was really doing: looking out and dreaming. He was seeing his descendants occupy the land in his heart. So, the question now is: what have you seen?

Psalm 145:19 AMP *He will fulfill the desires of those who reverently and worshipfully fear Him; He also will hear their cry and will save them.*

Chapter 6

Mysticism Unplugged

There are many misconceptions about calling and purpose. You could call them myths almost. It is simply religious notions that have caused confusion. If not addressed they can create doubt as you travel along the path to discovering your purpose. They sound reasonable at times; almost spiritual, mystical. As humans we often fall into the trap of not trusting what we hear God saying; whether that be directly to our hearts, or indirectly through others. We seek out signs to confirm the direction we are supposed to go in. There are two problems with that:

1. We are to act in faith, or trust. 2 Cor. 5:7[1]

2. We see signs that only confirm what we have already decided. It is called confirmation bias.

Religion and tradition rely on external signs rather than trusting the voice of the Lord in their hearts. I am not saying we should not look at situations around us. I am saying we should seek God's leading over those signs. External signs should be guide markers, not the GPS, so to speak. If the signs do not line up to the leading of our hearts they should be disregarded. Well-intentioned people, people with selfish intentions, and even satan, can set you off your course in this way.

2 Corinthians 11:14 CEV   And it is no wonder, even satan tries to make himself look like an angel of light.

Notice what Jesus said about signs:

Matthew 12:38-39 MontgomeryNT Then some of the Scribes and Pharisees accosted him. "Teacher," they said, "we want to see some sign from you." In reply Jesus told them. "An evil and faithless generation seeks a sign, and no sign will be given them except the sign of the prophet Jonah.

Matthew 16:1-4 MontgomeryNT   Then the Pharisees and Sadducees came to him, and in order to test him, asked him to show them a sign from heaven. In answer he said. "In the evening you say, 'It will be fine weather, for the sky is red as fire'; and at dawn you say, 'It will storm today, for the sky is red and lowering.' You know how to discern the look of the sky, but the signs of the times you cannot read. A wicked and faithless generation is seeking a sign, but no sign shall be given it but the sign of Jonah." So he left them and went away.

Luke 11:29 CEV As crowds were gathering around Jesus, he said: You people of today are evil! You keep looking for a sign from God. . .

Signs can be easily misinterpreted and manipulated. It boils down to this: do I trust God leading through my heart, or do I trust external signs? Again, signs should serve as guide markers. They should confirm what you already know in your heart. They will also line up with the keys we have discussed in previous chapters. There are so many variables regarding discovering purpose. There are absolutely guide markers along the way. Opportunities will come along. We want to take mysticism, religion, and tradition out of the equation.

*Mark 7:13 AMP Thus you are nullifying and making void and of no effect [the authority of] the Word of God through your **tradition**, which you [in turn] hand on.*

Led By The Spirit

Romans 8:14 AMP For all who are led by the Spirit of God are sons of God.

It comes down to being led by the Spirit of God. What is God saying to you? To where and what are you drawn? Honestly, it can be a very uncomfortable place, which we will see more in another chapter. But it is also the **safest** place, and the most fulfilling. It is a place of faith, not sight[2]. The tendency to rely on signs is opposite of what God asks of us.

Hebrews 11:6 MSG It is impossible to please God apart from faith.

God asks that we trust Him; His voice and His leading. Otherwise, we are constantly trying to interpret what we see around us. It will lead to a place of mysticism, where religion and tradition are trying to tell you which direction to go. Being led by the Spirit will help weed out things that would distract you. I have found that people led by the Spirit do not get caught up in external things. Rather they are led internally. They allow the inner life to interpret the external life, not the other way around.

*Luke 17:20-21 GW   The Pharisees asked Jesus when the kingdom of God would come. He answered them, "People can't observe the coming of the kingdom of God. They can't say, 'Here it is!' or 'There it is!' You see, the kingdom of God is **within you**."*

It will be contradictory, at times, to traditional thinking. Sometimes it won't make sense.

Does a door seem closed? Mysticism says God doesn't want you to go through it. It is closed for a reason. It is possible He might not want you to go through, but it is also possible He might want you to kick it down! Does a door seem open, an opportunity perhaps? Mysticism will say that is God making a way for you. It is open for a reason. God may tell you to not go through it. Close it! But He may tell you to walk through. Mysticism will say it is only God's purpose if everything lines up, if it is smooth sailing. Mysticism will say if it isn't hard, it is not God. The Spirit says none of that matters. What matters is what God says. Let's look at an example from the book of Acts. In Acts 16, we see Paul and Silas intending to go into a region to preach the gospel:

*Acts 16:6-7 NLT   Next Paul and Silas traveled through the area of Phrygia and Galatia, because the Holy Spirit had **prevented** them from preaching the word in the province of Asia at that time. Then coming to the borders of Mysia, they headed north for the province of Bithynia,but again the Spirit of Jesus **did*** *not allow* them to go there.

From a perspective of mysticism, religion, and tradition this seems odd. We are commanded to go into the world and preach the gospel[3]. But, we see in this case the Spirit would not allow them to do that. It is hard to understand why God leads a certain way. God sees things from a broader perspective than we do. That is why we must trust Him. External conditions and circumstances should not be the determining factor of what we do in following our purpose. We should be led by the Spirit.

*Psalm 143:10 CEV You are my God. Show me what you want me to do, and let your gentle Spirit **lead** me in the right path.*

*Acts 11:12 CEV The Holy Spirit **told** me to go with them ...*

*Acts 13:4 NLT So Barnabas and Saul were **sent** out by the Holy Spirit...*

Personal Responsibility

Laying down mysticism and being led by the Spirit requires personal responsibility. There is a misconception that if God calls you to something then all the responsibility lies with Him. Nothing could be further from the truth. We see this principle in Matthew 25:14-30[4], the parable of the talents. We also see it in Genesis 2:15[5], which we looked at earlier in the second chapter. God has entrusted us with a purpose and we are to take responsibility for that purpose. There is an eternal perspective with our purpose, and we should treat it seriously.

So, what is God's part in our purpose? It is simply to lead us and help us.

*Psalm 54:4 MSG   Oh, look! God's right here **helping**! God's on my side.*

*Psalm 54:4 AMP   Behold, God is my **helper** and ally; the Lord is my upholder and is with them who uphold my life.*

*Hebrews 13:6 NLT   So we can say with confidence, "The LORD is my **helper**, so I will have no fear. What can mere people do to me?"*

*Hebrews 4:16 KJV   Let us therefore come boldly unto the throne of grace, that we may obtain mercy, and find grace to **help** in time of need.*

Notice how Hebrews 4:16 says to come boldly unto the throne of **grace**. Grace means 'the divine influence on the heart'[6]. It can also mean 'to aid and assist'[7]. It is the ability of God influencing our heart to aid and assist us; to empower us to do what He has called us to do. That is His role in this; to help and empower. Our role is to walk it out. Let's look at some examples of this:

*Genesis 13:14-17 NLT   After Lot had gone, the LORD said to Abram, "Look as far as you can see in every direction—north and south, east and west. I am giving all this land, as far as you can see, to you and your descendants as a permanent possession. After Lot had gone, the LORD said to Abram, "Look as far as you can see in every direction—north and south, east and west. I am giving all this land, as far as you can see, to you and your descendants as a permanent possession. And I will give you so many descendants that, like the dust of the earth, they cannot be counted! **Go and walk through the land in every direction**, for I am giving it to you."*

We saw this account of Abram in the last chapter. After Abram looked in each direction God told him to walk through the land in every direction he had looked. By taking personal responsibility, Abram became established in his destiny. Each step Abram took reinforced the desire of his heart and reinforced that God would help him achieve it. We, likewise, have to be willing to put actions with faith[8]. It is how we establish our hearts in our purpose. There will always be opportunity to invest in your future through action. Then we can conclude what Abram did:

Romans 4:20-21 NLT   Abraham (Abram) never wavered in believing God's promise. In fact, his faith grew stronger, and in this he brought glory to God. He was fully convinced that God is able to do whatever he promises.

We see something similar with Moses and Joshua. After Moses brought the nation of Israel out of Egypt, the Lord gave Moses instructions for the people. Among those instructions was this exhortation:

Deuteronomy 11:24 BBE   Every place where you put your foot will be yours.

We then see the Lord saying this to Joshua after Moses died:

Joshua 1:2-3 BBE   Moses my servant is dead; so now get up! Go over Jordan, you and all this people, into the land which I am giving to them, to the children of Israel. Every place on which you put your foot I have given to you, as I said to Moses.

The principle here is 'everywhere **you** set your foot'. They had a responsibility. That responsibility was tied directly to their purpose.

They would be given the land that their feet touched. So, their future was limited only by their ambition and the actions they put with those ambitions. Dreaming without action is just wishing. Purpose not acted upon is just potential. We must assume personal responsibility over our purpose.

Chapter 7

Identity

Much of what I teach is about identity: being established in how God sees us. Being established in a God-sense of identity is vitally important as we discover our purpose. I touched on this in Chapter 2 regarding value and worth. We want to live our lives out of the identity we have in God. We do not use our purpose to establish our value and worth. Rather, we use our value and worth to establish our purpose. If we try to get value and worth from our purpose, we will be in a constant state of emotional turmoil and confusion. God does not love us because of our purpose. He gives us purpose because He loves us. Purpose should flow as a by-product of our identity. Purpose should never be the source of our identity. Our source of identity must be from God.

1 John 3:1 MSG   What marvelous love the Father has extended to us! Just look at it—we're called children of God! That's who we really are. . .

Romans 8:15-16 BBE   For you did not get the spirit of servants again to put you in fear, but the spirit of sons was given to you, by which we say, Abba, Father. The Spirit is witness with our spirit that we are children of God:

Ephesians 1:5 BBE   As we were designed before by him for the position of sons to himself, through Jesus Christ, in the good pleasure of his purpose,

Identity Releases Purpose

Purpose flows from a sense of identity. Identity frees us to make the choices to follow our purpose. Identity frees us from the care of reputation and criticism. It releases us to follow God's leading.

*Philippians 2:7-8 KJV   But made himself of **no reputation**, and took upon him the form of a **servant**, and was made in the likeness of men: And being found in fashion as a man, he **humbled** himself, and became **obedient** unto death, even the death of the cross.*

Jesus was obedient to His purpose by making Himself of 'no reputation'. He cast aside what others thought because He was established in His identity from the Father. Jesus did everything He did, including serving others, from His sense of identity.

*John 13:1-5 MSG   Just before the Passover Feast, Jesus knew that the time had come to leave this world to go to the Father. Having loved his dear companions, he continued to love them right to the end. It was suppertime. The Devil by now had Judas, son of Simon the Iscariot, firmly in his grip, all set for the betrayal. Jesus **knew** that the Father had put him in complete charge of everything, that he **came from God and was on his way back to God**. So he got up from the supper* *table, set aside his robe, and put on an apron. Then he poured water into a basin and began to wash the feet of the disciples, drying them with his apron.*

Being established in our God-given identity brings peace and rest to us as we pursue our purpose. Purpose is realized by being at rest in our identity. Rest and peace will keep condemnation from paralyzing us when we make a mistake. It helps us get back up when we fall.

Proverbs 24:16 AMP For a righteous man falls seven times and rises again. . .

The word 'righteous' here, when applied from a New Testament perspective, is speaking of identity. We are righteous in Jesus[1]. We have been given the free gift of righteousness, right standing with God[2]. Why can a righteous man fall and rise again? It is because a righteous man is established in his God-given identity. He sees himself through the lens of God's value which was demonstrated through the death, burial, and resurrection of Jesus[3]. A person established in righteousness knows God is for them. Life will throw hard things at us. We must get up and keep going.

It ain't how hard you hit. It's how hard you can get hit and keep moving forward. It's about how much you can take and keep moving forward!" — Sylvester Stallone, Rocky Balboa

Abram vs. Abraham

In Genesis 12, we are introduced to Abram. Abram's name means 'exalted father'[4]. We follow Abram's story; then we come to Genesis 17. In this chapter we see the Lord tell Abram, exalted father, that He is going to change his name to Abraham, which means 'father of a multitude, or many'[5]. God changed Abram's name **before** he actually became a father of many. In fact, Abram had only one child at that time: Ishmael, whom he had fathered with his wife's handmaid, Hagar[6]. God's promise was that Abram would become a father of many with his wife, Sarai, who became Sarah, which means princess[7]. Abram was ninety-nine years old when God changed his name[8]. We then see in Genesis 21 that Abraham had a child, Isaac, with his wife, Sarah. When Isaac was born, Abraham was one hundred years old[9].

That means that Abram was introducing himself as Abraham for a year before Isaac was born! His servants were calling him Abraham. His wife was calling him Abraham. Every time he heard that name, his *expected end* was being established in his heart. God established his purpose through his identity, his name! He called himself 'father of many'. Others called him 'father of many'. Purpose flowed from his identity! When we embrace who we are in Jesus, as we become established in the identity given to us by God, purpose will flow from that. We will be assured that he has given us a 'hope and a future'[10]. We will be convinced that God will help us reach that destiny[11].

Chapter 8

The Road Ahead

Although finding your purpose may seem difficult, it is simply the first step in your journey. The road ahead can be as equally difficult, if not more so in some ways. Once you have found your purpose, and you walk in that purpose, there will always be decisions to make. There will be situations ahead that you must confront. That is one reason I am so adamant about you being established in identity and being confident in your purpose. When faced with these things, it is easy to lose heart and quit. In the gospels, Jesus spoke about the 'parable of the sower'[1]. He gave insight to how we can be drawn away from the things of God so easily if our hearts are not established in His word.

Something to remember about purpose and calling is that it is not absolute, even though it is from God. You have an *expected end*, but that does not mean it is automatic. It is an *expected end*, not a guaranteed end. Remember what I said from the first chapter: there are lots of people through the ages who went to their graves not fulfilling their purpose. There are those who perverted their purpose as well. Fulfilling your purpose is a day to day conscious decision. It is gained by tedious attention to detail. It is gained through a tenacious desire to see it through until the end. History does not write itself. We write history. Sometimes, contrary to religious thinking, God does not always get His way; at least with each of us individually. Usually, it is because we are in His way.

Alternative Destiny

Although the destiny of God is not absolute, you will fulfill some sort of destiny if not established in the purpose and identity of God. It will be the destiny that others choose for you. It will be the result of what they speak over you, should you allow yourself to listen. It will be the by-product of their limitations on you, should you allow yourself to be swayed by that. Other people, and their ideas for your life, are a serious deterrent to the purpose God has for you. Sometimes it is intentional, sometimes it is not. Either way, the result is the same.

Galatians 4:17 KJV   They zealously affect you . . .

In this verse, the phrase 'zealously affect' can also mean 'to be moved with envy toward' or 'covet'[2]. In this phrase, we see three types of people. One type is envious but doesn't bear ill intent. They are like crabs stuck in a bucket. When one crab tries to climb out, the others will drag him back down. They have gotten comfortable in their situation. Anyone who breaks rank makes them uncomfortable. I have found it is usually because they then must face why they are still stuck in the bucket. The second type is envious, but they intentionally want to hold you back. They don't want you to achieve what they feel they can't achieve. Instead of finding joy for you, all they give off is negativity in their words and actions towards you.

Proverbs 10:11 MSG The mouth of a good person is a deep, life-giving well, but the mouth of the wicked is a dark cave of abuse.

One thing to remember is that not everyone will be happy with your dreams. We saw this in Chapter 3 with Moses, but let's look at another story we looked at in Chapter 5, the story of Joseph:

Genesis 37:10-11 MSG When he told it to his father and brothers, his father reprimanded him: "What's with all this dreaming? Am I and your mother and your brothers all supposed to bow down to you?" Now his brothers were really jealous; but his father brooded over the whole business.

Genesis 37:19 AMP And they said one to another, See, here comes this dreamer and master of dreams. (author's note- sarcasm)

Notice the disbelief, the jealousy, and the sarcasm from Joseph's family. When you find your purpose not everyone will agree with you. Some will be jealous. Some will mock you. When I started pursuing my purpose there were plenty of people who mocked me, made fun of me. Some of those people were other believers, brothers and sisters in Jesus. Joseph's brothers wanted to kill him! They eventually sold him into slavery over their jealousy. There will be some who will try to enslave you, using your gifts and calling for their own benefit. This is the third type of person.

Galatians 4:17 Phillips NT   Oh, I know how keen these men are to win you over, but can't you see that it is for their own ends?

Instead of seeing the bigger picture of God's plan and purpose, they have a limited view of the kingdom of God. It is usually limited to their scope of influence. They have no desire for you other than how you can help fulfill their agenda. By doing this they can also limit the vision in your heart and make you feel like it is the right thing! They covet your gifts so they can use them to further their own purposes without considering the cost to the kingdom. We should never allow ourselves to serve other people's purpose at the expense of our own. They should work in a synergistic fashion where each contributes to the other.

These are just a few ways we can get caught up in an alternative destiny. Another way is to believe what others say to us and about us. The saying 'Sticks and stones will break my bones, but words will never hurt me' is a lie. Words follow us. We can put off from our minds things said to us, and then out of the blue something will trigger the memory. We live it all over again. I can remember the hurt of words much clearer than I can remember physical hurt. Don't let anyone rob you of your dreams! Become established in your God-given identity so you can recognize these things. Set them away from you.

Isaiah 54:17 CEV   Weapons made to attack you won't be successful; words spoken against you won't hurt at all. . .

*1Isaiah 54:17 KJV   No weapon that is formed against thee shall prosper; and every tongue that shall rise against thee in judgment thou shalt **condemn**. . .*

Self-Perception

Among these scenarios, we have to discuss our own self-perception. Not only can we fulfill an alternative destiny of other people, but we can also fulfill an alternative destiny through poor self-perception. The words we say about ourselves can actually cause more damage than what others say. Why? Because we are with ourselves all of the time! Again, this is why it so important to be established in the identity you have in Jesus. You can talk yourself out of your purpose. You can disqualify yourself in your own heart by what you think and say about yourself. Jesus paid a great price for you. What He says about you should be what you say about you. You are a pearl of great price[3]! What you think and say about yourself will place you on one of two paths: the path to fulfill your *expected end*, or the path to negative self-fulfilling prophecy.

*Proverbs 4:23 NLT   Guard your heart above all else for **it determines the course of your life.***

We are to condemn words that rise against us in judgment, including our own. We must see ourselves the way God does. We see ourselves through the lens of the obedience of Jesus. He was obedient to death to make us sons of God! We must bring every thought and every word to that. That is how we guard our heart from ourselves.

The Road Ahead

2 Corinthians 10:5 KJV   Casting down imaginations, and every high thing that exalteth itself against the knowledge of God, and bringing into captivity every thought to the obedience of Christ;

Every thought and every word you say about yourself has to be given this test: does this thought or these words line up to the conclusion that Jesus' obedience brought to me? What was the conclusion of His obedience? He made us children and brought us into glory, or dignity and worth[4]. Is it pride to see ourselves as God does? No, it is humility. We are changing our thoughts to His thoughts. Sometimes, we just must get out of our own way.

Chapter 9

Seeing It Through

Once you have identified your purpose, and begin the steps to walk it out, commit to seeing it through. Be diligent even when things seem stagnant. Sometimes things will seem dry and mundane. Times when it seems like all of your efforts are for nothing. In these times you must press on. In these times you are refined and being transformed into the image of Jesus, the image He has of you and your *expected end*. In diligence we see our purpose come to pass.

Proverbs 28:20 KJV   A faithful man shall abound with blessings. . .

Hebrews 6:11 NIV   We want each of you to show this same diligence to the very end, so that what you hope for may be fully realized.

Proverbs 12:24 KJV   The hand of the diligent shall bear rule: but the slothful shall be under tribute.

One definition of the word 'diligence' in Proverbs 12:24 above is 'to trench'[1]. We are to be so faithful we are entrenched, nothing can move us. It is diligence, or faithfulness, that creates opportunity. Contrary to religion and tradition, it is not that our faithfulness **earns** us anything; He freely gives us all things[2]. It is simply that being faithful and obedient leads us to the places God has for us.

*Isaiah 1:19 NKJV   If you are **willing and obedient**, You shall eat the good of the land;*

It is not a magic trick, or a test of some kind. He is not withholding something from you until you get it right or stay at it long enough. It is simply that God sees from a higher perspective. He knows if we stay a certain course it will take us right into the path of opportunity. It is not a wage to be earned, but what we find because of listening to His voice and acting upon it. It goes back to something we saw in the first chapter: the law of serendipity. So, if it is not God keeping it from us, why do we still miss the prize? It is usually because we quit too soon.

*Romans 12:11 CEV   **Never give up.** Eagerly follow the Holy Spirit and serve the Lord.*

*Galatians 6:9 KJV   And let us not be weary in well doing: for in due season we shall reap, **if we faint not.***

*Hebrews 12:1 NIV   Therefore, since we are surrounded by such a great cloud of witnesses, let us throw off everything that hinders and the sin that so easily entangles. And let us run with **perseverance** the race marked out for us,*

Remember that God is faithful. Even when we make a mistake, He is faithful. Even when we want to give up, He is faithful. Make a wrong turn? Do not quit and remember He is faithful.

2 Timothy 2:13 NLT   If we are unfaithful, he remains faithful, for he cannot deny who he is.

Hebrews 6:10 KJV   For God is not unrighteous to forget your work and labour of love. . .

He wants you to reach your *expected end*. He is the one who gave it to you. God has a stake in your destiny. He set you over the works of His hand[3].

Letting The Past Pass

A major deterrent to seeing our purpose through is the past. Humans hang on to past hurts, failures, and mistakes. We judge ourselves based on things that happened in the past. Much of the time we decide our worthiness and value based on past events. Your value and worth have nothing to do with your past. God's opinion of you does not change based on your past. His gifts and calling are irrevocable; they never change[4]. In God's view those things never happened.

Psalm 103:12 NLT He has removed our sins as far from us as the east is from the west.

Micah 7:19 NLT   Once again you will have compassion on us. You will trample our sins under your feet and throw them into the depths of the ocean!

Hebrews 8:12 MSG   They'll get to know me by being kindly forgiven, with the slate of their sins forever wiped clean.

We must let go of our past failures. Maybe you have made some mistake and you think that mistake has disqualified you from your calling. Maybe certain situations or circumstances have convinced you that pursuing your dream is useless. Let me assure you that is not true! You must find your purpose; both for you and for the kingdom of God. God has a plan for you, and it is permanent and eternal. God has placed a purpose inside of you. He will never give up on you; no matter how long it takes.

Rom. 11:29

NCV *God never changes his mind about the people he calls and the things he gives them.*

KJV *For the gifts and calling of God are without repentance.*

Even though Moses killed another man[5], God did not change His mind about him or his purpose. God is not withholding our *expected end* from us; **we** are not taking hold of it in our hearts. God is calling us into our purpose; but because of our insecurities and fears we run from Him and His purposes. The same thing happened to Moses and it cost him forty years[6].

We also must let go of the hurts others have caused us as well. I know it is easier said than done. If we continue to hold on to those past hurts it only limits us and our future. You will react to present situations through the lens of pain from the past. It will cause turmoil and will create roadblocks on the path of purpose. Forgive those who have hurt you. Let go of any slight, perceived or real. You cannot change it and it will affect your future if you hang on to it. Instead, focus on your own growth. Focus on the fact that God is for you[7]. Learn from those past hurts, your self-inflicted wounds, and the pain others have caused. Just don't let it limit you, or paralyze you, or define you.

Philippians 3:13-14 BBE. . . but one thing I do, **letting go** *those things which are* **past***, and stretching out to the things which are* **before***, I go forward to* **the mark***, even the* **reward of the high purpose of God in Christ Jesus***.*

Hebrews 12:1 NIV   Therefore, since we are surrounded by such a great cloud of witnesses, let us throw off everything that hinders and the sin that so easily entangles. And let us **run** *with perseverance* **the race** *marked out for us*

I love what Hebrews 12:1 says above in the NIV. Throw off everything that hinders, and the sin that entangles. The word 'entangles' in the KJV is 'beset'[8]. In the Greek, it means 'to thwart' [9]. Throw off everything that thwarts you and that comes against you to throw you off your purpose. Anything that would hinder you in pursuit of God's purpose needs to go. That ranges from negative self-perception, the expectations of others imposed upon you, unjust criticism, negative self-talk, hurtful words of others, and your own past actions. Let it go and see it through!

Chapter 10

Of Like Passions

As we have seen, we can allow limitations from other people. We can allow limitations from within ourselves. We can allow the past to create limitations on our purpose. In the same way we can also allow limitations of our purpose by looking too harshly on our present condition: our maturity or lack thereof. We sometimes have the misconception we have to reach a certain level of maturity to do things God has called us to do. As we progress through our journey we must grow and mature at each level of that journey. However, we should not be paralyzed into inaction. We must start somewhere, regardless of maturity. Here is a simple truth of the kingdom of God: God works through imperfect people.

James 5:17-18 KJV Elias (Elijah) was a man subject to like passions as we are, and he prayed earnestly that it might not rain: and it rained not on the earth by the space of three years and six months. And he prayed again, and the heaven gave rain, and the earth brought forth her fruit.

The Montgomery NT translates 'to like passions' as 'of like passions'[1]. Other translations say Elijah was human just like us. The Greek defines 'subject to like passions' as *being similarly affected*[2]. He was imperfect. He experienced everything we do. He sinned, just like we do. He failed at times, just like we do. Yet James 5:17-18 says he prayed once for it to stop raining, and it stopped. Then he prayed for it to rain and it rained[3]. He was called to be a prophet to Israel. That was his purpose. His imperfections did not negate his calling. Do not disqualify yourself from your purpose based on your condition. God will transform you as you go. He will equip you as you walk along the path of your journey. That is part of being led by the Spirit.

2 Corinthians 3:18 KJV But we all, with open face beholding as in a glass the glory of the Lord, are **changed into the same image from glory to glory** *(author's note-step by step), even as by the* **Spirit** *of the Lord.*

There are plenty of examples of this in the Bible:

- Moses killed a man[4].

- Samson was a fornicator[5].

- David was an adulterer and murderer[6].

- Solomon was a polygamist[7].

Look at Abraham from the book of Genesis. He had a laundry list of failings. He slept with his wife's handmaiden to bear a child[8]. He disobeyed God when God told him to leave his father's house and family by taking his nephew, Lot, with him[9]. He lied to the pharaoh of Egypt by saying his wife Sarah was his sister to keep from being killed[10].

In these situations, God did not take their purpose away due to their shortcomings. He led them into it despite their shortcomings. They grew as they went. There is not a magic level to achieve before you are qualified to pursue your destiny. God may instruct you to prepare for the next level. He may give you a course of action to take before the next step. But He is not saying do not start. We grow from glory to glory. Each step of the journey prepares us for the next step. We need not be perfect to pursue our purpose. We simply must have a heart that will yield to God.

The 'Peter' Factor

One of Jesus' twelve disciples, those closest to Him, was Peter. Peter was a strong personality and was highly emotional. In Matthew 26, we read the account of Jesus' arrest[11]. Before the arrest Jesus told His disciples they would all fall away and disown Him before the night was out. Peter said he would stay loyal even if the others fell away. Jesus told Peter that before the rooster crowed three times Peter would deny Him. Peter responded by saying he would die before he would deny Jesus[12]! As Jesus was brought before the chief priests, Peter was asked three times, by different people, if he was a disciple of Jesus. Each time Peter replied "No". When the third denial came the rooster crowed[13]. This was the same man who told Jesus he would not deny Him even if the others denied Him. This is the same man who said he would die before denying Jesus. We see in John 18:26[14] that this was the same man who cut off the ear of one of the soldiers that came to arrest Jesus. Yet he is denying Jesus in this account.

After Jesus' death, burial, and resurrection He shows Himself to His disciples. In John 21, we read a conversation between Jesus and Peter[15]. Jesus asks Peter three times "Do you love me?" Each time Peter said "Yes, Lord". Each time Jesus told Peter to feed and tend His sheep[14]. Even after Peter denied Him, the Lord still had purpose for Peter. Regardless of where you are, where you have been or what you have done, God is not through with you. If He was not done with Peter, He is not done with you. We simply must be willing to allow Him to lead the way and allow Him to change us along the way. His grace is sufficient.

2 Corinthians 12:9 NIV   But he said to me, "My grace is sufficient for you, for my power is made perfect in weakness." Therefore I will boast all the more gladly about my weaknesses, so that Christ's power may rest on me.

2 Corinthians 4:7 NIV   But we have this treasure in jars of clay to show that this all-surpassing power is from God and not from us.

Chapter 11

A Place of Rest

Jeremiah 29:11 KJV   For I know the thoughts that I think toward you, saith the LORD, **thoughts of peace**, *and not of evil, to give you an expected end.*

There is a paradox concerning pursuing our purpose. The paradox is this: we must strive and work towards our purpose yet remain at peace internally. Truthfully, if you are serious about pursuing your purpose, the work never ends. That does not mean you must be in turmoil internally. You will see more results when your heart and mind are at peace. We saw in Chapter 3 that hope is the anchor for our mind, will and emotions: our soul[1]. An anchor keeps us stable while the waves of life crash all around us. Stability brings peace and rest to our being. Our peace cannot be an artificial construct based on emotions or circumstances; it must come from God.

In the verse that started this chapter, Jeremiah 29:11, we can see His thoughts towards us are peace. The peace He has towards us needs to resonate within us and be established in our hearts. The way He thinks about us is crucial to pursuing our purpose from a place of rest.

Philippians 4:7 MontgomeryNT and the peace of God, which passes all understanding, will stand guard over **your hearts and your thoughts** *in Christ Jesus.*

It becomes the difference between being busy or being fruitful, productive. A person at rest in their heart will produce more than someone who strives. They won't be distracted by busy work or appearance. Being in rest or being in strife comes down to motive. The actions may look the same, but the intent is entirely different. A person who strives in their heart is always busy trying to earn God's approval. Because of that they cannot slow down long enough to hear God. Their sole aim is to get God to respond to them. A person whose heart is at rest is simply responding to God, not trying to get Him to respond. A heart that is in a place of rest can hear what God is saying.

Psalm 46:10 NIV He says, "Be still, and know that I am God. . .

A Pliable Heart

Psalm 37:4 NKJV Delight yourself also in the LORD, And He shall give you the desires of your heart.

Regarding being at rest in our hearts, this verse takes on a different application than in Chapter 5. The word 'delight' in this verse means *to be pliable, soft*[2]. What God desires is for us to have a heart that is pliable, or willing to be molded and transformed. Remember, He is the potter and we are the clay[3]. The only way for us to have a soft and pliable, or flexible, heart is to be at rest in His peace towards us. Only then will we allow Him to shape us and mold us into our purpose. Look at these scriptures that caution us not to harden our hearts when we hear His voice:

Hebrews 3:7-8 NLT That is why the Holy Spirit says, **"Today when you hear his voice, don't harden your hearts** *as Israel did when they rebelled, when they tested me in the wilderness.*

Hebrews 3:15 BBE As it is said, Today if **you will let his voice come to your ears, be not hard of heart,** *as when you made him angry.*

Hebrews 4:7 NKJV again He designates a certain day, saying in David, "Today," after such a long time, as it has been said: **"Today, if you will hear His voice, Do not harden your hearts."**

These verses are so close together and all in the context of rest! Because of the hardening of their hearts an entire generation of the nation of Israel missed out on entering their promised land, their *expected* end[4]. I am absolutely convinced that a pliable heart is necessary to find and walk in our purpose. A pliable heart is flexible to shift and change as God reveals more to us about our purpose. Remember in Chapter 5, I mentioned that God giving us the desires of our heart works two ways: first, He puts the desire in us; then second, He brings us the desire. I also mentioned that tradition and religion say that whatever you do not want to do is what God wants you to do. Scripture says He gives us the (good) things our hearts desire. But, given the definition of 'delight' there is something else at play here. Let's say you have no desire to teach a Bible class. But you want to honor God and keep a pliable heart. Through that flexibility of heart, He puts in you, over time, the desire to teach. He gives you the desires of your heart!

I have seen this in my own life over the years. I would be walking in my purpose as I knew it at the time. But, as I continued to commune with God more of His plan was revealed. There are inherent desires we are born with inside of us. He put those there, or gave those, even before we were in the womb[5]. Those form the hub of the wheel we saw in Chapter 1. But the spokes, the extended purpose, come from that intimate communion with God that can only come from a heart in a place of rest. The full scope of our purpose comes through a soft, flexible heart. A pliable heart will allow God to place His desires inside of us. Then His desires become our desires. He does not make us do anything we have no desire to do. He simply creates the desire within us. Then we follow Him in it. That enabled Jesus to follow through at the cross even after asking if there was any other way[6]. A pliable heart, surrendered to God, seeks His will and His purpose. It allows Him to transform us and speak purpose to us. I said it in the last chapter and I will say it again: we need not be perfect to pursue our purpose. We simply must have a heart that will yield to God. He is the potter and we are the clay; it will be a joy to us.

The Burden of Purpose

There is great responsibility in finding, and walking in, our purpose. It is a sobering, serious issue with eternal ramifications. But, when done from a place of rest and with a soft heart the burden of purpose will not weigh us down. Even the things we suffer as we walk out our purpose will seem mild compared to the end result.

Romans 8:18 GW I consider our present sufferings insignificant compared to the glory that will soon be revealed to us.

*Matthew 11:28-30 NKJV Come to Me, all you who labor and are heavy laden, and I will give you rest. Take My yoke upon you and learn from Me, for I am gentle and lowly in heart, and you will find **rest** for your souls. For My yoke is easy and My burden is light."*

Notice what Jesus says in the verse above: His burden is easy and light. Even when the work required is hard, the burden is light. Work and burden are two different things. Work is the mental and physical toil required to produce anything in life. A burden is something that takes a toll on us emotionally and spiritually. The place we want to be, and God asks us to be, is where the work does not become a burden. This all comes from a place of rest. If it ever seems that the burden of purpose is a weight on your heart or on your mind, it is not God. It could be a misapplication in how we are walking out our purpose. We saw that with Abraham in regard to Hagar and Ishmael[7]. Abraham's wife, Sarah, convinced Abraham that God's promise would come through him conceiving a child with Hagar. It did not end well. Anything that takes us off the path of our purpose will weigh us down and wear us out. The blessing of the Lord does not add sorrow (painful toil, grievous labor)[8].

Matthew 23:4 NKJV   For they bind heavy burdens, hard to bear, and lay them on men's shoulders; but they themselves will not move them with one of their fingers.

Our purpose cannot come from a place of trying to prove ourselves. It cannot come from comparing ourselves to others. It cannot come from trying to please others or trying to earn God's pleasure. It must come from a place of rest.

*Hebrews 4:9-11 NKJV There **remains** therefore a **rest** for the people of God. For he who has entered His rest has himself also ceased from his works as God did from His. Let us therefore **be diligent to enter that rest**, lest anyone fall according to the same example of disobedience.*

Chapter 12

Counting The Cost

Luke 14:28 NKJV For which of you, intending to build a tower, does not sit down first and count the cost, whether he has enough to finish it--

As we begin the journey towards our purpose we have to consider the cost. Any endeavor in life comes at a price. What will be required of you in this pursuit of God's purpose for your life? I have had to make decisions of how to spend my time, my money, and any other resources to better position myself for God's calling. I have had to remove myself from situations and people that caused me to be distracted. I still have to make those decisions. They are not always easy. My body and mind does not always want to wake up early to pray and commune with God. My mind does not always want to sit at my desk and study. I do not always want to take the time and energy to push through writer's block. The first thing required in pursuit of purpose is discipline.

There will be times when you have to do things that you do not want to do, at least at that particular time. I can remember studying for my theology degree. The program was available as correspondence so I opted for that instead of moving my young family on campus for residency. I worked 60 hours a week, and I was also the youth pastor of the church we attended. There was so much going on: family activities, my children's sports and school events, work, church, etc. I did not always want to sit down and work through a class. I wanted to rest! But I knew that to be equipped for my calling I had to be disciplined to do the work in spite of everything else going on around me. I was up early in the morning, even on the weekends. Once I came home from work and said hello to everyone I allotted an hour and a half daily to do course work. After that was spent with my family: helping with the kids' schoolwork, dinner, and just hanging out. I knew that during that hour and a half I had to be focused. It was not always easy. I did not always want to do it, but the reward at the end of it was sweet.

Discipline towards our purpose never goes away. There will always be something that needs to be done. There will always be times we would rather be doing something else. Of course we can enjoy ourselves. Not every waking moment has to be work, work, work. The Father wants you to enjoy life. You will know when to push and when to back off. That is the beauty of being led by the Spirit. Always remember there should be balance, even in discipline. Be disciplined, but not consumed. Proverbs 11:1 says that a false balance is abomination, or idolatry, to the Lord; but a just weight is His delight[1].

Secondary Gains

We need to able to put aside things that would distract us from our purpose. That becomes harder when a secondary gain is attached to those things. A secondary gain is any benefit we receive or perceive that we receive from behavior, habits, hobbies, relationships, etc. The concept of secondary gain is used in the medical and psychological field primarily. It is used to describe positive advantages that are obtained incidentally through illness. The concept can apply to anything to which we attach value and anything by which we receive value, real or perceived.

One aspect of counting the cost is to evaluate those secondary gains. Does the value we receive from those things outweigh the value of pursuing our purpose and calling? Remember, Proverbs 11:1 says a false balance is an abomination to the Lord. One meaning of 'abomination' is *destructive to harmony*². Placing secondary gains above purpose can be destructive to the harmony in your life. It can cause a false balance. We may gain a secondary benefit, but our heart will never be satisfied until the primary purpose of our lives becomes more valuable than any secondary gain.

Proverbs 13:12 AMP   Hope deferred makes the heart sick, but when the desire is fulfilled, it is a tree of life.

The Trap of Offense

One aspect of counting the cost is in the area of emotions and ego. Our emotions and ego will suffer temporary bruising from time to time. The biggest enemy of emotions and ego is the trap of offense. Jesus said it is impossible but that offense will come. One definition of offense is *resentment brought about by an insult or disregard for oneself or one's standards or principles*[3] (real or perceived). The trap of offense is that it leads to bitterness. Bitterness can cause us to remove ourselves from the path of purpose. How do we deal with offense and not let it affect our purpose? Jesus shows us in these verses:

Luke 17:1 KJV   Then said he unto the disciples, It is impossible but that offences will come....

Luke 17:3 KJV   ......Take heed to yourselves.....

Jesus said that when offense comes that we should take heed to ourselves. We look at our response. We look at why we are offended. We determine not to shift blame or let any offense take root. We take responsibility. The quickest way to bitterness in our heart is to let offense fester. When we allow our emotions to dwell on an insult or slight, real or perceived, then offense has become the rudder of our ship. It has become our god.

Proverbs 19:11 AMP   Good sense makes a man restrain his anger, and it is his glory to overlook a transgression or an offense.

When we overlook an offense we are ensuring that our heart does not become hard and bitter. The truth is it is rare that someone offends us on purpose. Most people do not know where you are in your heart. Only you can determine that. Most of the time, it is just an indicator of where they are in maturity. Does that mean that we never confront bad behavior? No! It means that even when confronting bad behavior we refuse to allow it to determine our response. We have to count the temporary hurt to our emotions and ego as insignificant to the cost of bitterness that could lead us to leaving our purpose.

Suffering Reproach

Hebrews 11:24-26 KJV   By faith Moses, when he was come to years, refused to be called the son of Pharaoh's daughter; Choosing rather to suffer affliction with the people of God, than to enjoy the pleasures of sin for a season; Esteeming the reproach of Christ greater riches than the treasures in Egypt: for he had respect unto the recompence of the reward.

In this passage of scripture we see that Moses chose to suffer affliction rather than enjoy the treasures of Egypt. It says he esteemed the reproach, or defamation[4], of His calling as greater than the Egyptian treasure and position. The word 'esteeming' in this passage means *to deem, consider, count, to lead, and to have the rule over*[5]. Moses counted the cost and deemed the reproach and the affliction of being with his people as greater than the position, power, and treasure that being the son of the pharoah's daughter would bring to him. I find it interesting that 'esteeming' can also mean *to have the rule over* and *to lead*. This basically means that what Moses considered after counting the cost was what led him and gave him direction; the counting of the cost had the rule over his life. The reproach was of little consequence when viewed alongside of the reward for following his purpose.

The Gap

If we do not stand resolute in being disciplined, on putting aside distractions, not allowing offense to hinder us, and suffering reproach then we run the risk of being put off the path of purpose. This does not only affect us. It affects the entire body of Christ. In Romans 12 and 1 Corinthians 12, Paul compares the body of Christ to the human body. He says that no part of the body can say to any other part that there is no need of you. The human body works in balance. When one part of the body is hurt or ill it affects the rest of the body. If one part of the body is not doing what it is created to do then the whole body is thrown off balance. If one part of the body suffers, it can cause damage to other parts of the body. I am sure we have all seen, or experienced, where one issue in our body causes an over-reliance on another part of our body to compensate for the part that is hurting, or lacking. I have a family member who had trouble with her hips which in turn caused trouble in her knees which in turn caused trouble in her feet. Pretty soon, arthritis developed in those major joint areas.

It is the same way in the body of Christ. If we remove our gifts, our calling, and our purpose from the body then other members have to pull up the slack. That in turn causes too much pressure on the other members of the body to try and supply the missing part, our part. Paul comes to this conclusion:

1 Corinthians 12:25 KJV That there should be no schism in the body; but that the members should have the same care one for another.

The word 'schism' means *a split, a gap*[6]. When we remove our part the body suffers a gap. The church suffers a gap. You are important to the body of Christ in more ways than you can imagine; not from an arrogant or haughty perspective, but from a perspective of the value God has placed on you. In the same way the human body gets off balance when one member is not doing its part, so does the church get off balance. Find your part. Count the cost.

1 Corinthians 12:25 MSG The way God designed our bodies is a model for understanding our lives together as a church: every part dependent on every other part....

Chapter 13

Life On Purpose

Each of us has an *expected end*. We are given gifts and talents to help us reach our intended destination. Purpose is a gift from God; second only to salvation and communion with God that Jesus secured for us on the cross. It is a blessing to us to be given purpose. But, the reason for our purpose is not just for us. Our purpose accomplishes a part of God's plan for His kingdom. Our purpose affects others as well. We must see the bigger picture in our purpose. Although we will reap the benefits of purpose, it really is not about us.

*Genesis 12:2 NKJV   I will make you a great nation; I will **bless you** and make your name great; And **you shall be a blessing**.*

We are blessed with purpose to be a blessing to others. He will bless you and **make** you a blessing. That is the ultimate goal of purpose: to be made a blessing. Will we find contentment and satisfaction? Yes! Are there benefits to walking in our purpose? Yes! But the greatest result is being made a blessing to others.

Life On Purpose

The Law of Inertia

So, what do we do until we know our purpose? I believe we live life **on** purpose. Choose to live a life in pursuit of purpose. Choose to commune with God each day. Choose to be a blessing right now. You can begin that right now, right where you are. It is the law of inertia: an object in motion stays in motion. It takes more force to start an object moving than it does to change its course. If you are already in motion, God can change your direction quicker and easier than He can get you started. From a heart perspective, a heart living on purpose will find the way to its intended destination much easier.

The key is to simply start. When I was trying to find my core purpose, I started by scrubbing toilets. That is where I started. I would clean the church once a week. I made reading my Bible a daily habit. I greeted people at the door. I was involved on the worship team, and in ushering. I got in motion. During this time the Lord showed me the principles I am sharing with you now. I was already in motion and my heart was determined to live on purpose. It made it easier for me to hear God. Just start!

The Ministry of Reconciliation

One mistake Christians make is thinking that finding their purpose means going into ministry. Anything that serves others is technically ministry. But, when finding purpose is talked about it seems we default to thinking about becoming a pastor, or evangelism. God has called, and will call, His people to different arenas of life. Some will find purpose in things not necessarily within the church: business, sports, entertainment, etc. There is one ministry, however, that we are all called to fulfill. Whether we have found our purpose or not, we are all called to the ministry of reconciliation.

2 Corinthians 5:18-21 NKJV Now all things are of God, who has reconciled us to Himself through Jesus Christ, and has given us the ministry of reconciliation, that is, that God was in Christ reconciling the world to Himself, not imputing their trespasses to them, and has committed to us the word of reconciliation. Now then, we are ambassadors for Christ, as though God were pleading through us: we implore you on Christ's behalf, be reconciled to God. For He made Him who knew no sin to be sin for us, that we might become the righteousness of God in Him.

That is the purpose of all believers; a universal purpose apart from personal purpose. We are to tell others that God has brought reconciliation to mankind, restoring the relationship broken by Adam's sin[1]. To tell others that God is no longer holding anything against them. Jesus was the offering, once for all[2], for our sin. The thing in the way between us and God has been removed, and we now have right standing with God. That is the ministry of reconciliation. It is the purpose of the church and of each of us individually.

Life On Purpose

Excuses, Excuses, Excuses

One pitfall of the human experience is the tendency to want to blame others and make excuses. It has been that way since the fall of man in the Garden of Eden[3]. If we are to walk in our purpose, we must let go of any excuse that prevents us from moving forward. We see in the account of Moses, in the books of Exodus and Acts, some of the excuses we use to justify not pursuing our purpose, or to avoid the responsibility of purpose. In Exodus 3, God called Moses out of Midian to go and deliver the Israelites out of Egypt. Exodus 4 begins with Moses telling God that the Israelites will not believe that God has sent him to them. Moses believed he was not qualified. What was God's response?

Exodus 4:2-9 NLT   Then the LORD asked him, "What is that in your hand?" "A shepherd's staff," Moses replied. "Throw it down on the ground," the LORD told him. So Moses threw down the staff, and it turned into a snake! Moses jumped back. Then the LORD told him, "Reach out and grab its tail." So Moses reached out and grabbed it, and it turned back into a shepherd's staff in his hand. "Perform this sign," the LORD told him. "Then they will believe that the LORD, the God of their ancestors—the God of Abraham, the God of Isaac, and the God of Jacob—really has appeared to you." Then the LORD said to Moses, "Now put your hand inside your cloak." So Moses put his hand inside his cloak, and when he took it out again, his hand was white as snow with a severe skin disease. "Now put your hand back into your cloak," the LORD said. So Moses put his hand back in, and when he took it out again, it was as healthy as the rest of his body. The LORD said to Moses, "If they do not believe you and are not convinced by the first miraculous sign, they will be convinced by the second sign. And if they don't believe you or listen to you even after these two signs, then take some water from the Nile River and pour it out on the dry ground. When you do, the water from the Nile will turn to blood on the ground."

In the same way, we often feel unqualified for what we are called to do; not enough education, not enough money, not enough influence, afraid of what others will think. But, just as Moses, God will make a way. God responded to Moses' fear of being unqualified, not good enough, by making a way for him. We no longer have the excuse of being unqualified. He has qualified us. Are there things we may need to do to help us have more credibility? Yes, and He will show you that as well. But, ultimately, we must conclude that His call is the qualifier. Even when others would try to disqualify you, remember, God will make a way.

The next thing we see in Exodus 4 is Moses saying to God he is not an eloquent speaker. He had a speech impediment (slow of speech and tongue[4]). He had a physical limitation. It is easy for us to lose sight of our purpose when we have a physical limitation. It can be any type of limitation: physical, financial, etc. What was God's response to Moses?

Exodus 4:11-16 NKJV   So the LORD said to him, "Who has made man's mouth? Or who makes the mute, the deaf, the seeing, or the blind? Have not I, the LORD? Now therefore, go, and I will be with your mouth and teach you what you shall say." But he said, "O my Lord, please send by the hand of whomever else You may send." So the anger of the LORD was kindled against Moses, and He said: "Is not Aaron the Levite your brother? I know that he can speak well. And look, he is also coming out to meet you. When he sees you, he will

Life On Purpose

be glad in his heart. Now you shall speak to him and put the words in his mouth. And I will be with your mouth and with his mouth, and I will teach you what you shall do. So he shall be your spokesman to the people. And he himself shall be as a mouth for you. . .

Once again, God made a way. He would teach Moses what to say. Even then, Moses tried to get out of being sent. So, once again, God made a way. He made Moses' brother Aaron his spokesman. Moses believed his limitations would not allow him to do what God had called him to do. We do the same thing. We look at our limitations and our circumstances. We decide that we can't possibly do what we are supposed to do. The situation is overwhelming. But God will make a way. God loves to do things with us that in the natural does not seem probable. We no longer have the excuse of limitations.

2 Corinthians 12:8-10 NLT   Three different times I begged the Lord to take it away. Each time he said, **"My grace is all you need. My power works best in weakness."** *So now I am glad to boast about my weaknesses, so that the power of Christ can work through me. That's why I take pleasure in my weaknesses, and in the insults, hardships, persecutions, and troubles that I suffer for Christ. For when I am weak, then I am strong.*

We see another excuse we use from the account of Moses in Acts 7. We have already seen in another chapter that Moses killed an Egyptian that was beating a fellow Hebrew. When he learned that others knew about it, he fled into Midian. Acts 7:23 said Moses was forty years old when this happened. We know from Exodus that Moses married and settled in Midian[5]. Acts 7:30 says Moses was in Midian for forty years when the Lord appeared to him in the burning bush.

That means Moses was eighty years old when God called him to go back to Egypt. Eighty years old! How often has purpose been derailed because we think age is a factor? Age is not a factor with God. Purpose does not disappear at a certain age. God does not change His mind. We no longer have the excuse of age.

Romans 11:29 AMP For God's gifts and His call are irrevocable. [He never withdraws them when once they are given, and He does not change His mind about those to whom He gives His grace or to whom He sends His call.]

It is never too late to be what you might have been. —George Eliot

Final Thoughts

Some of you reading this may already know your purpose. My prayer and hope is that this has encouraged you to see it through. If you have laid it down, for whatever reason, I want to encourage you to pick it back up, right where you are. Some of you may have been walking in your purpose, and this has simply been a tool to help you expand that vision, to be open to other possibilities, more spokes. Some of you may have never even considered that you have a purpose. I hope this has inspired you to begin the journey and process of pursuing your purpose. There will be challenges. There will be delays. There will be times when you must be patient, when everything in you screams 'Now!' There will be times you will need to heed advice, and times to not heed advice.

There may be some discomfort, but God does not take me out of where I am comfortable just for the sake of making me uncomfortable. Any time God moves us into areas we have never been there will be discomfort and apprehension. The discomfort is not about us individually. It is about His Kingdom. Unfortunately, there is no magic wand, or universal template. It is one of the things I love about walking with God: no two journeys are exactly alike. It is a walk of faith, of trust. Just remember, He knows the end from the beginning[7]. God is for you, and so am I.

Romans 8:31-32 NIV   What, then, shall we say in response to these things? **If God is for us, who can be against us?** *He who did not spare his own Son, but gave him up for us all—how will he not also, along with him, graciously give us all things?*

Psalm 20:4 NKJV   May He grant you according to your heart's desire, **And fulfill all your purpose.**

Bibliography

Chapter 1

1. Proverbs 4:23

2. If the heart is sick, it can lead to physical sickness. It is psycho-somatic.

3. Acts 7:23-30 Moses was 40 when he killed the Egyptian, responding to God's call. He fled to Midian and was there 40 years when the Lord appeared to him in the burning bush.

4. Jeremiah 29:11 (NLT)

Chapter 2

1. Strong's Concordance- yāsar

2. Strong's Concordance- ābad

3. Strong's Concordance- shāmar

4. This is a quote from Psalm 8:5. In Psalm 8:5, the word for 'angels' is *Elohim* which means gods, or supreme god (Strong's Concordance). This implies that we are created a little lower than the Godhead.

5. Strong's Concordance- episkeptomai Thayer's Greek-English Lexicon- "to look upon in order to help or to benefit, equivalent to look after, have a care for, provide for, to furnish with things necessary

6. Strong's Concordance- doxa, timē

7. Luke 4:8   Jesus is quoting Deuteronomy 6:13 and 10:20 . He replaces the word 'fear' with 'worship'. In both verses in Deuteronomy the word 'fear' is : Strong's Concordance- yārē. Brown-Driver-Briggs Hebrew-English Lexicon- pay reverence to. Luke 4:8 'worship' is: Strong's Concordance- proskyneō . Thayer's Greek-English Lexicon- to kiss the hand to (toward) one, in token of reverence. See also 1 John 4:18

8. Genesis 3:8

9. Genesis 3:12

10. Matthew 6:26-30

11. Genesis 1:31

Chapter 3

1. Strong's Concordance- Hebrew: tiqwâ, Greek: elpis Thayers Greek-English Lexicon-much more frequent in the classics, and always in the N.T., in a good sense: expectation of good, hope"

2. Thayer's Greek-English Lexicon-the seat of the feelings, desires, affections, aversions

3. Romans 8:31

4. Exodus 18:13-16 (KJV) And it came to pass on the morrow, that Moses sat to judge the people: and the people stood by Moses from the morning unto the evening. And when Moses' father in law saw all that he did to the people, he said, What is this thing that thou doest to the people? why sittest thou thyself alone, and all the people stand by thee from morning unto even?And Moses said unto his father in law, Because the

people come unto me to enquire of God:When they have a matter, they come unto me; and I judge between one and another, and I do make them know the statutes of God, and his laws.

5. Exodus 3:11-4:17

Chapter 4

1. Strong's Concordance- māshâ

2. Acts 7:25

3. Exodus 2:15, Acts 7:29

Chapter 5

1. Strong's Concordance- nātan

2. Strong's Concordance- yāsar, Vine's Expository Dictionary of Old and New Testament Words-to form, mold, fashion

3. Strong's Concordance- nātan

4. Strong's Concordance- qādash

5. Strong's Concordance- yāda

6. Strong's Concordance- nāhâ, Brown-Driver-Briggs Hebrew-English Lexicon- lead, guide

7. Proverbs 16:9 (NIV) In their hearts humans plan their course, but the LORD establishes their steps.

8. Genesis 42:6 (NIV) Now Joseph was the governor of the land, the person who sold grain to all its people. So when Joseph's brothers arrived, they bowed down to him with their faces to

the ground.

9. Genesis 43:26 (NIV) When Joseph came home, they presented to him the gifts they had brought into the house, and they bowed down before him to the ground.

10. Proverbs 16:9 (NKJV)

11. 1 Timothy 3:1

12. Psalm 37:4

Chapter 6

1. 2 Corinthians 5:7 (KJV)   For we walk by faith, not by sight:

2. 2 Corinthians 5:7

3. Matthew 28:18, Mark 16:15

4. Matthew 25:14-30 (KJV) For the kingdom of heaven is as a man travelling into a far country, who called his own servants, and delivered unto them his goods.And unto one he gave five talents, to another two, and to another one; to every man according to his several ability; and straightway took his journey.Then he that had received the five talents went and traded with the same, and made them other five talents. And likewise he that had received two, he also gained other two.But he that had received one went and digged in the earth, and hid his lord's money.After a long time the lord of those servants cometh, and reckoneth with them. And so he that had received five talents came and brought other five talents, saying, Lord, thou deliveredst unto me five talents: behold, I have gained beside them five talents more.His lord said unto him, Well done, thou good and faithful servant: thou hast been faithful

over a few things, I will make thee ruler over many things: enter thou into the joy of thy lord. He also that had received two talents came and said, Lord, thou deliveredst unto me two talents: behold, I have gained two other talents beside them. His lord said unto him, Well done, good and faithful servant; thou hast been faithful over a few things, I will make thee ruler over many things: enter thou into the joy of thy lord. Then he which had received the one talent came and said, Lord, I knew thee that thou art an hard man, reaping where thou hast not sown, and gathering where thou hast not strawed: And I was afraid, and went and hid thy talent in the earth: lo, there thou hast that is thine. His lord answered and said unto him, Thou wicked and slothful servant, thou knewest that I reap where I sowed not, and gather where I have not strawed: Thou oughtest therefore to have put my money to the exchangers, and then at my coming I should have received mine own with usury. Take therefore the talent from him, and give it unto him which hath ten talents. For unto every one that hath shall be given, and he shall have abundance: but from him that hath not shall be taken away even that which he hath. And cast ye the unprofitable servant into outer darkness: there shall be weeping and gnashing of teeth.

5. Genesis 2:15 (NKJV) Then the LORD God took the man and put him in the garden of Eden to tend and keep it.

6. Strong's Concordance- charis

7. Thayer's Greek-English Lexicon- the aid or succor (help) of divine grace, attends and assists one.

8. James 2:17 (KJV) Even so faith, if it hath not works, is dead, being alone.

Chapter 7

1. 2 Corinthians 5:21 (NIV)   God made him who had no sin to be sin for us, so that in him we might become the righteousness of God.

2. Romans 5:17-18 (NKJV) For if by the one man's offense death reigned through the one, much more those who receive abundance of grace and of the gift of righteousness will reign in life through the One, Jesus Christ.)   Therefore, as through one man's offense *judgment* came to all men, resulting in condemnation, even so through one Man's righteous act *the free gift came* to all men, resulting in justification of life.

3. Romans 5:8 (KJV) But God commendeth his love toward us, in that, while we were yet sinners, Christ died for us.

4. Strong's Concordance- abrām: *high father; Abram*, the original name of Abraham.

5. Strong's Concordance- abrāhām: *father of a multitude; Abraham*, the later name of Abram

6. Genesis 16:1-4

7. Genesis 17:15

8. Genesis 17:1

9. Genesis 21:5

10. Jeremiah 29:11 (NIV) For I know the plans I have for you," declares the LORD, "plans to prosper you and not to harm you, plans to give you hope and a future.

11. Hebrews 13:6, Psalm 54:4

Chapter 8

1. Matthew 13:1-23, Mark 4:1-20, Luke 8:4-15

2. Strong's Concordance- zēloō

3. Matthew 13:45-46

4. Hebrews 2:10

Chapter 9

1. Strong's Concordance- chârûts

2. Romans 8:32 (KJV)   He that spared not his own Son, but delivered him up for us all, how shall he not with him also freely give us all things?

3. Hebrews 2:7 (NKJV) You have made him a little lower than the angels; You have crowned him with glory and honor, And set him over the works of Your hands.

4. Romans 11:29 (NKJV)   For the gifts and the calling of God *are* irrevocable.

5. Exodus 2:11-12

6. Acts 7:30

7. Romans 8:31 (KJV) What shall we say then to these things? If God be for us, who can be against us?

8. Hebrews 12:1 (KJV) Wherefore seeing we also are compassed about with so great a cloud of witnesses, let us lay aside every weight, and the sin which doth so easily beset *us*, and let us run with patience the race that is set before us.

9. Strong's Concordance- euperistatos

Chapter 10

1. James 5:17 (MontgomeryNT)   Elijah was a man of like passions with us, and he prayed again, and the sky gave rain, and the earth brought forth her fruit.

2. Strong's Concordance- homoiopathēs

3. 1 Kings 17:1, 1 Kings 18:41-45

4. Exodus 2:11-12

5. Judges 16:1

6. 2 Samuel 11:1-17

7. 1 Kings 11:3

8. Genesis 16:1-4

9. Genesis 12:1-5

10. Genesis 12:11-20

11. Matthew 26:47-57

12. Matthew 26:33-35

13. Matthew 26:69-75

14. John 18:26 (KJV) One of the servants of the high priest, being his kinsman whose ear Peter cut off, saith, Did not I see thee in the garden with him?

15. John 21:15-17

Chapter 11

1. Hebrews 6:19 (NLT) This hope is a strong and trustworthy

anchor for our souls. It leads us through the curtain into God's inner sanctuary.

2. Strong's Concordance- ānag, Brown-Driver-Briggs Hebrew-English Lexicon-soft, delicate, dainty, make soft, pliable

3. Isaiah 64:8, Jeremiah 18:1-7

4. Joshua 5:6

5. Jeremiah 1:5

6. Matthew 26:39, 42, Luke 22:42

7. Genesis 21:9-11

8. Proverbs 10:22 (KJV) The blessing of the LORD, it maketh rich, and he addeth no sorrow with it. Strongs Concordance-eseb

Chapter 12

1. Proverbs 11:1 (KJV) A false balance *is* abomination to the LORD: but a just weight *is* his delight.

2. Strong's Concordance-toeba, Vine's Expository Dictionary of Old and New Testament Words- characteristics are destructive of societal and familial harmony; disrupting unity and harmony.

3. Oxford English Dictionary

4. Strong's Concordance-oneidismos: from the root oneidizō, to defame, chide, taunt, upbraid

5. Strong's Concordance-hēgeomai

6. Strong's Concordance-schisma

Chapter 13

1. Romans 5:19

2. 2 Corinthians 5:19-21, Hebrews 7:27, Hebrews 10:10

3. Genesis 3:12

4. Exodus 4:10

5. Exodus 2:16-22

ABOUT THE AUTHOR

Randall Rittenberry lives in Cookeville, Tennessee with his wife, Cynthia. Since 1995, he has served as a counselor, pastor, and teacher. He has served in, and developed, ministries within the local church including: helps (ushers and greeters), children's ministry, youth ministry, and worship. He has held leadership and administrative positions in churches, and also a national ministerial organization. He has a passion to help people develop to their full potential, and to see themselves the way God sees them. For more info go to:

www.randallrittenberry.com

You can find teaching resources there such as videos, podcasts, and articles.

Made in the USA
Monee, IL
22 August 2021

75555087R00059